Idaho

By Pam Zollman

Subject Consultant
Robert Goodrich, Lecturer
University of Idaho
Moscow, Idaho

Reading Consultant
Cecilia Minden-Cupp, PhD
Former Director of the Language and Literacy Program
Harvard Graduate School of Education
Cambridge, Massachusetts

Children's Press®
A Division of Scholastic Inc.
New York   Toronto   London   Auckland   Sydney
Mexico City   New Delhi   Hong Kong
Danbury, Connecticut

Designer: Herman Adler Design
Photo Researcher: Caroline Anderson
The photo on the cover shows Idaho's Big Wood River and Sawtooth Mountains.

Library of Congress Cataloging-in-Publication Data

Zollman, Pam.
 Idaho / by Pam Zollman.
  p. cm. — (Rookie read-about geography)
 Includes index.
 ISBN 0-516-24965-7 (lib. bdg.)   0-516-26609-8 (pbk.)
 1. Idaho—Juvenile literature. 2. Idaho—Geography—Juvenile literature. I. Title.
II. Series.
 F746.3.Z64 2006   2005026250
 979.6—dc22

JE
ZOL
C.1   6/07

CHILDREN'S PRESS, and ROOKIE READ-ABOUT®,
and associated logos are trademarks and/or registered trademarks
of Scholastic Library Publishing. SCHOLASTIC and associated logos
are trademarks and/or registered trademarks of Scholastic Inc.

1 2 3 4 5 6 7 8 9 10 R 15 14 13 12 11 10 09 08 07 06

Idaho has three regions. They are the Rocky Mountain, Columbia Plateau, and the Basin and Range regions.

The Basin and Range Region

The Rocky Mountain Region has tall mountains, deep canyons, and swift rivers. A canyon is a deep valley cut by a river.

The Rocky Mountains cover most of Idaho. Thick forests grow in this region.

Hell's Canyon is the deepest canyon in North America. It is part of the Rocky Mountain Region.

The Snake River runs
through Hell's Canyon.
It is Idaho's longest river.

The Snake River Plain is in the Columbia Plateau Region. A plateau is high, flat land.

Most people in Idaho live in the Columbia Plateau Region. It is a good place to grow potatoes and sugar beets. Idaho is famous for its potatoes.

The Basin and Range Region has grassy plateaus and deep valleys. Small mountain ranges cut through this region.

There are farms in the valleys. Cattle graze on the mountain slopes.

Boise is the capital of Idaho. It is also the state's largest city. Idaho is the 11th-largest state in the United States.

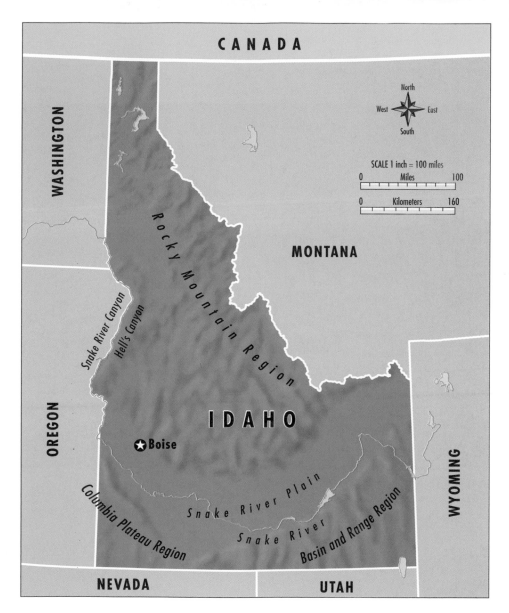

CANADA

WASHINGTON

MONTANA

North
West ✦ East
South

SCALE 1 inch = 100 miles

0   Miles   100

0   Kilometers   160

Rocky Mountain Region

Snake River Canyon

Hell's Canyon

IDAHO

OREGON

⭐ Boise

Columbia Plateau Region

Snake River Plain

Snake River

Basin and Range Region

WYOMING

NEVADA

UTAH

An Idaho silver mine

Mining is important work in Idaho. People dig up sand, gravel, copper, zinc, and silver. Idaho has the three richest silver mines in the United States.

Jade, opal, and garnet are gems that are mined in Idaho. A gem is a precious stone. Idaho's state gem is the star garnet.

Star garnet

A wolf

Idaho is home to many different types of wildlife. Moose, wolves, badgers, and mink live there.

Bald eagles, loons, and wild turkeys also live in Idaho. The state bird is the mountain bluebird.

25

Winters in Idaho are cold. It snows a lot in the mountains. People like to go skiing, sledding, and ice-skating.

Idaho summers are hot.
People enjoy hiking and
camping. They also like to
swim and fish.

What would you like to
do in Idaho?

29

Words You Know

Columbia Plateau

Hell's Canyon

mountain bluebird

potatoes

Rocky Mountains

star garnet

31

Index

About the Author

Pam Zollman is an award-winning author of short stories and books for kids.
She's a native Texan who now lives in the Pocono Mountains of Pennsylvania.
Pam dedicates this book to Christina Dodd Ham, a fellow writer and close friend
who revels in the beauty of Idaho.

Photo Credits

Photographs © 2006: Alamy Images/Steve Platzer/Stock Connection Distribution:
9, 31 bottom right; Corbis Images: 3 (Dean Conger), 7 (Ric Ergenbright), 11
(Dave G. Houser), 27 (Karl Weatherly), 22 (Jim Zuckerman); Dembinsky Photo
Assoc./Mary Liz Austin: cover; Folio, Inc./Richard Nowitz: 10, 30 bottom; Getty
Images/Harry Taylor: 21, 31 top right; Houserstock/Steve Bly: 29; ImageState/
Andy Anderson: 26; Photo Researchers, NY: 6, 30 top (Ted Clutter), 13, 14, 18,
31 bottom left (David R. Frazier); Superstock, Inc./T. Vandersar: 25, 31 top left.

Maps by Bob Italiano